PHONICS
BOOK TWO

A Workbook for Ages 4–6

Written by Vicky Shiotsu
Illustrated by Lucy Helle

LOWELL HOUSE JUVENILE

LOS ANGELES

NTC/Contemporary Publishing Group

Published by Lowell House
A division of NTC/Contemporary Publishing Group, Inc.
4255 West Touhy Avenue, Lincolnwood (Chicago), Illinois 60712 U.S.A.

Managing Director and Publisher: Jack Artenstein
Director of Publishing Services: Rena Copperman
Editorial Director: Brenda Pope-Ostrow
Director of Art Production: Bret Perry
Senior Educational Editor: Linda Gorman

Lowell House books can be purchased at special discounts
when ordered in bulk for premiums and special sales.
Please contact Customer Service at the above address,
or call 1-800-323-4900.

Printed and bound in the United States of America

ISBN: 0-7373-0499-5

RCP 10 9 8 7 6 5 4 3 2 1

GIFTED & TALENTED® WORKBOOKS will help develop your child's natural talents and gifts by providing activities to enhance critical and creative thinking skills. These skills of logic and reasoning teach children **how** to think. They are precisely the skills emphasized by teachers of gifted and talented children.

Thinking skills are the skills needed to be able to learn anything at any time. Unlike events, words, and teaching methods, thinking skills never change. If a child has a grasp of how to think, school success and even success in life will become more assured. In addition, the child will become self-confident as he or she approaches new tasks with the ability to think them through and discover solutions.

GIFTED & TALENTED® WORKBOOKS present these skills in a unique way, combining the basic subject areas of reading, language arts, and math with thinking skills. The top of each page is labeled to indicate the specific thinking skill developed. Here are some of the skills you will find:

- Deduction—the ability to reach a logical conclusion by interpreting clues
- Understanding Relationships—the ability to recognize how objects, shapes, and words are similar or dissimilar; to classify or categorize
- Sequencing—the ability to organize events, numbers; to recognize patterns
- Inference—the ability to reach a logical conclusion from given or assumed evidence
- Creative Thinking—the ability to generate unique ideas; to compare and contrast the same elements in different situations; to present imaginative solutions to problems

GIFTED & TALENTED® WORKBOOKS have been written and endorsed by educators. These books will benefit any child who demonstrates curiosity, imagination, a sense of fun and wonder about the world, and a desire to learn. They will open your child's mind to new experiences and help fulfill his or her true potential.

This book is designed to give children an opportunity to play with and explore the sounds of the letters of the alphabet. This study of the letter sounds is known as **phonics**.

Almost every page asks the child to write or draw in response to the challenge or question presented. This helps to put the task of working with letters in context. The importance of phonics lies in its ability to help us to understand and express language, so in addition to decoding, the child is expected to demonstrate understanding and practice expression. If this proves difficult for your child, don't be afraid to help. Encourage him or her to talk through the responses while thinking them through. If your child has not yet mastered writing, allow him or her to dictate longer answers while you write them. Write slowly, and let your child watch as you form the letters. Together, read back your child's own words.

The activities should be done consecutively, as they become increasingly challenging as the book progresses. Notice that on many pages, there is more than one right answer. Accept your child's response and then challenge him or her to come up with another. Also, where the child is asked to write, remember that the expression of his or her ideas is more important than spelling. At this age, the child should be encouraged to record the letter sounds that he or she hears without fear of mistakes. This process is known as **invented spelling**. If children only write words they know they can spell correctly, they will limit their written expression. Using invented spelling permits your child's spoken vocabulary to be available to him or her for writing.

For example, if your child writes *dnosr* for *dinosaur*, that's okay! Praise your child for the sounds he or she heard. You can encourage the child to listen for the missing vowels as you say the word and write it out so that the child can see the correct form. Just keep the emphasis on his or her success—the letters your child did hear—and not on his or her "error."

Reference charts depicting the sounds of letters appear on the next few pages. Help your child use the charts whenever he or she needs a reminder.

Consonant Chart

b ball

h horn

c cat

j jar

d dog

k kite

f fish

l leaf

g girl

m mouse

n nest

p pig

q queen

r ring

s sun

t turtle

v vase

w wagon

x X ray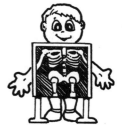

y yo-yo

z zebra

Short Vowel Chart

Short Vowel Sounds at the Beginning of Words	**Short Vowel Sounds in the Middle of Words**

a ant

a bat

e egg

e bell

i igloo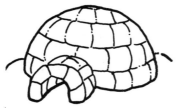

i mitt

o octopus

o fox

u umbrella

u duck

Long Vowel Chart

Long Vowel Sounds at the Beginning of Words	**Long Vowel Sounds in the Middle of Words**

a acorn

a cake

e eagle

e jeep

i ice

i bike

o ocean

o rope

u unicorn

u tube

Benny's Bugs

Can you find Benny's bugs? They are standing beside things that begin with **b**. Color Benny's bugs. Then color the things that begin with **b**.

Below, draw another bug that belongs to Benny. Beside it, draw something that begins with **b**. Write **b** on the line.

Cocoa's Castle

A creature named Cocoa lives in this castle. To find out what Cocoa is, color the spaces. If a space shows something that begins with **c,** color it blue. If it doesn't, color it yellow.

What kind of creature is Cocoa? _____

Dale's Dollhouse

Look at Dale's dollhouse. Trace the letter **d** at the top. Then color the things that begin with **d**.

Draw two more things in the dollhouse that begin with **d**.

Finish Frank's Pictures

Help Frank finish the pictures. Draw the pictures so that they match the words.

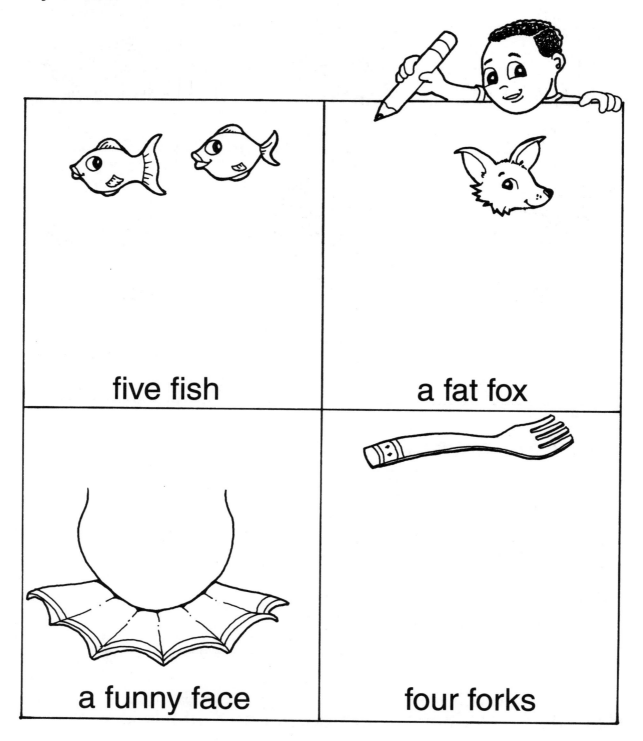

five fish

a fat fox

a funny face

four forks

Words With G

Look at the pictures and read the words. Then look at the shapes below. Write each word inside its matching shape.

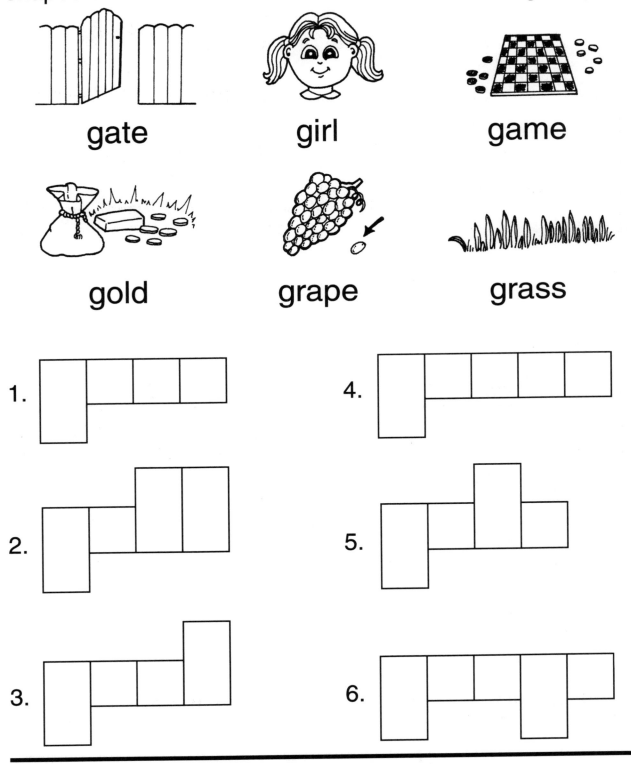

gate   girl   game

gold   grape   grass

1.

2.

3.

4.

5.

6.

Here's Harry!

Read the sentences in the box. Circle the words that begin with **h**.

> Harry has a hat on his head.
>
> He has a hammer in his hand.
>
> He is standing by his house.

Here is Harry. Complete the picture to match the sentences in the box.

Jay the Juggler

Jay likes to juggle. He also likes the letter **j**! Trace the **j** on Jay's hat. Then write **j** on the balls. Read the words you made.

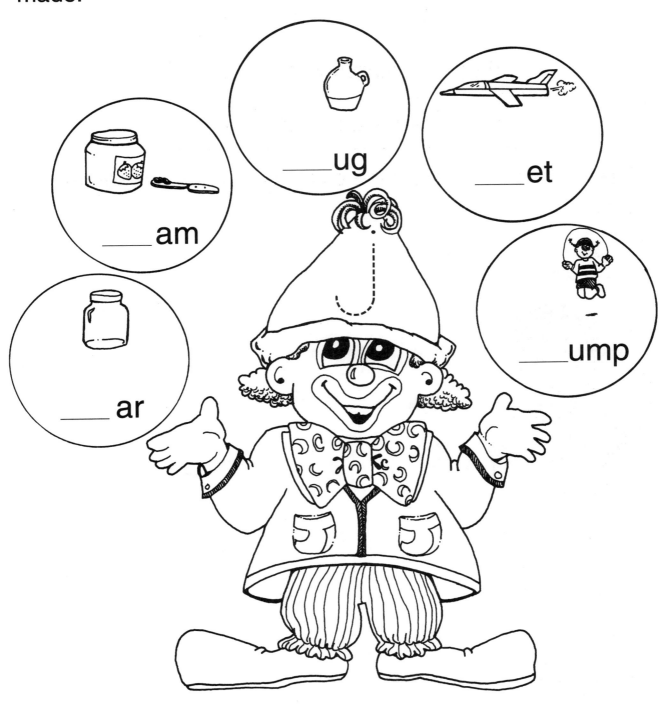

____ug

____et

____am

____ump

____ar

Katie's Kitchen

Look at Katie's kitchen. Find five things that begin with **k**. Color them red. Then color the rest of the picture any way you like.

Lulu's Lookout

Lulu is in her lookout tower. She is looking for things that begin with **l**. She sees a lamp and a log. Draw at least three other things that begin with **l**.

Words With M

Write **m** on the lines below. Then read the words aloud.

_____ug

_____itten

_____ask

_____oth

Decorate the pictures any way you like.

Nellie's Nest

Nellie Bird needs to get to her nest. Make a path for her by coloring the pictures that begin with **n**.

Plenty of Pies

Look at the pictures on each pie. Color the ones that begin with **p**.

Look at all the pictures again. How are the pictures in each pie alike? Say your answers aloud.

Questions With Q

Read the questions below. Say the names of the pictures as you read. Answer by writing **yes** or **no**.

Does begin with **q**? _____

Does begin with **q**? _____

Does begin with **q**? _____

Does begin with **q**? _____

Does begin with **q**? _____

Make up two more questions like the ones above. Let one question have **yes** for an answer and the other question have **no** for an answer. Ask your questions out loud.

Randy Rabbit

Randy Rabbit is walking along the road. He is picking up objects that begin with **r**. Trace the **r** on Randy's bag. Then circle the things that Randy will pick up.

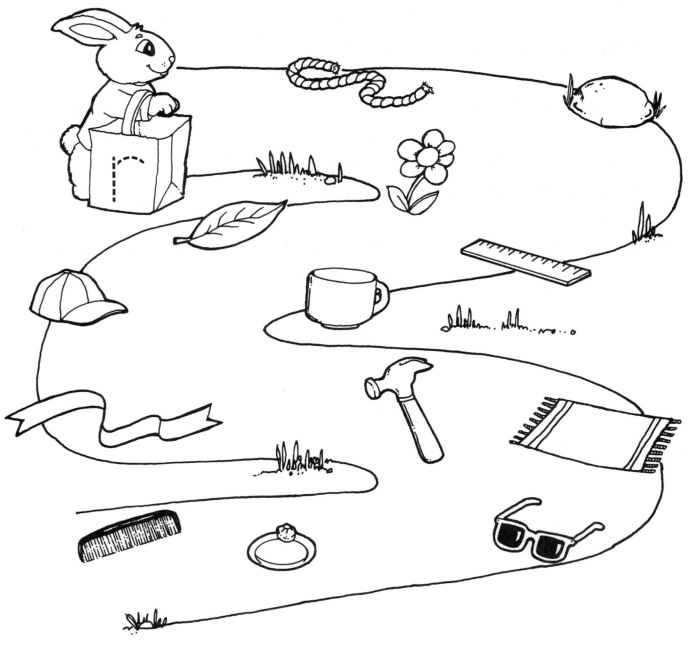

Which circled object is used to measure things? Color it yellow.

Sue's Socks

Read the sentences in the box. Circle the words that begin with **s**.

> Sue has six socks.
>
> Some socks have spots.
>
> Some socks have stripes.
>
> There are more socks with spots than socks with stripes.

Draw Sue's socks. Make them match the sentences in the box. Then color your picture.

A Camping Trip

Find seven things that begin with **t**. Color them green. Then color the rest of the picture any way you like.

Which **t** things do you usually find in a bathroom? Circle them.

Words With V

Write **v** on the lines below. Then read the words aloud.

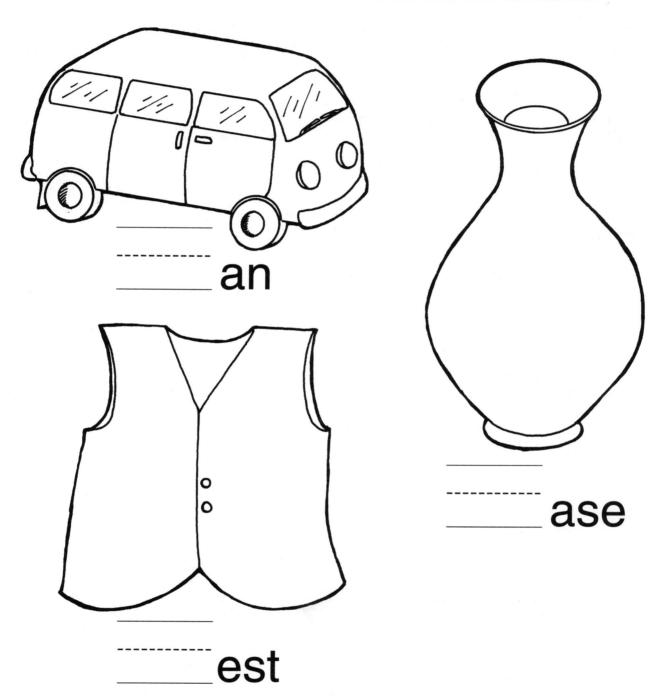

_____ an

_____ ase

_____ est

Decorate the pictures any way you like.

Walter's Wagon

Walter likes to carry things in his wagon. He carries only things that begin with **w**. Right now he is carrying a walrus and a wig. Draw at least three other things Walter can carry.

Look for X

Doctor Max is looking at an X ray. The word **X ray** begins with **x**. Look for the letter **x** in the picture. There are six of them. Color each **x** blue. Then color the rest of the picture.

Something Yummy

Read the poem. Circle the words that begin with **y**.

A yak named Yogi had a treat.

It was yellow. It was sweet.

"Thank you, Mom," said Yogi Yak,

"For making such a yummy snack!"

What kind of snack do you think Yogi Yak had? Draw your answer on the table. Then color your picture.

Words With Z

Read the sentences in the box. Circle the words that begin with **z**.

Zeke is a zebra.

He lives at the zoo.

He likes to wear clothes that have zippers.

What kinds of clothes have zippers? Draw some below.

Listen Carefully

Say the names of the pictures. Circle the letter you hear at the beginning of each word.

t r	n k	j s
d h	z p	y m
l x	f q	g d
z v	b l	w c

Look again. How are the three pictures in each row alike? Say your answers aloud.

Consonant Castle Game

Play this game with a friend. Place two markers on **Start**. Take turns flipping a coin. Move your marker one space for heads and two spaces for tails. Each time you land on a letter, say a word that begins with that letter. The first player to reach the Consonant Castle wins!

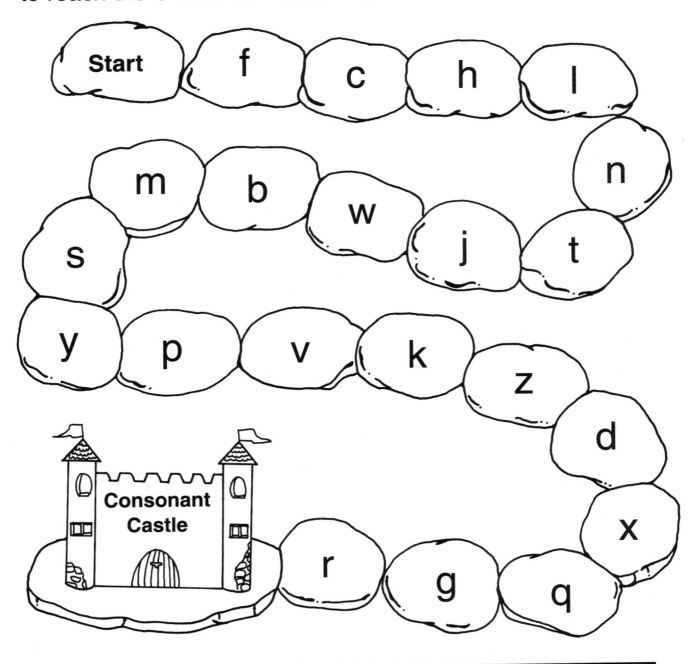

Playtime Fun

Say the names of the toys. Circle the letter you hear at the end of each word.

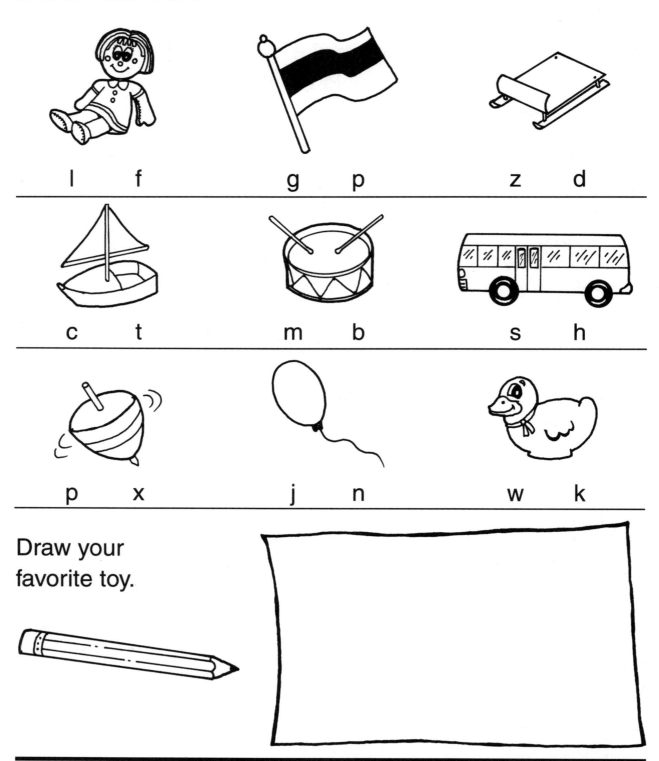

l   f   g   p   z   d

c   t   m   b   s   h

p   x   j   n   w   k

Draw your favorite toy.

Puzzle Challenge

Write a letter in each blank to make words that can be read across → and down ↓. Use the pictures to help you.

1.

h	
e	
v	a

3.

	c
	a
p	o

2.

	l
	o
p	i

4.

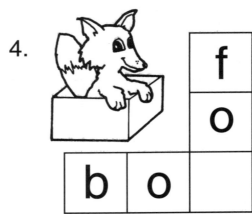

	f
	o
b	o

Write the words you made.

_____

- -

_____

- -

_____

Make up a story about one of the pictures. Tell the story to a parent or a friend.

Pop the Balloons

Help the clown write the word for each picture. Use the letters on the balloons to fill in the blanks. Cross out the letters as you use them and "pop" the balloons.

Think and Draw

Read the words. Draw pictures to match.

an animal that begins with **d**	an animal that ends with **t**
a food that begins with **b**	a food that ends with **n**
something in your home that begins with **w**	something in your home that ends with **k**

Shop With Ann

Ann is going shopping with her big bag. She wants to buy things that have short **a** in their names. The words **Ann** and **bag** have the short **a** sound. Look below. Color the things Ann will buy.

Which short **a** things can you wear? Circle them.

Jack's Sack

Read the words on Jack's sack. Listen to the short **a** sound in each word. Then write the words in the puzzle. Use the picture clues to help you.

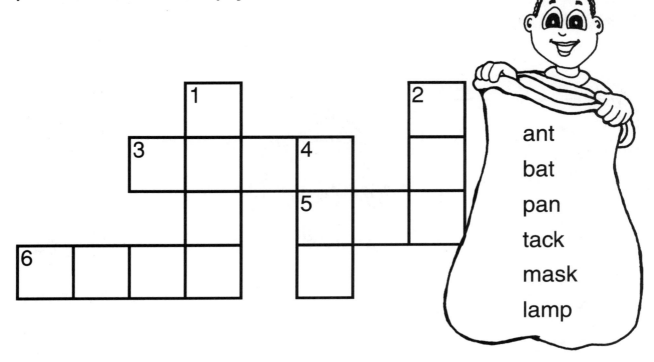

ant

bat

pan

tack

mask

lamp

Across

3.

5.

6.

Down

1.

2.

4.

Listen for Short E

Some words have the short **e** sound, such as **red**. Say the names of the pictures below. If a space shows something with short **e** in its name, color it red. If not, color it blue. When you are done, you will see something else that has short **e** in its name.

Brett's Pet

Read the poem. Circle the words that have short **e**.

Here is Brett.

He has a pet.

His pet named Fred

Is resting in bed.

What kind of pet do you think Brett has? Show your answer by drawing Brett's pet in bed.

Fish in a Dish

There are three fish in each dish below. The words **fish** and **dish** have the short **i** sound. Say the names of the pictures on the fish. Color each fish that has a picture of something with short **i** in its name.

Look at each dish and the fish you colored. Say the names of the pictures. How are the names alike?

Short I Riddles

Look at the pictures. Say the words aloud. Listen to the short **i** sound in each name.

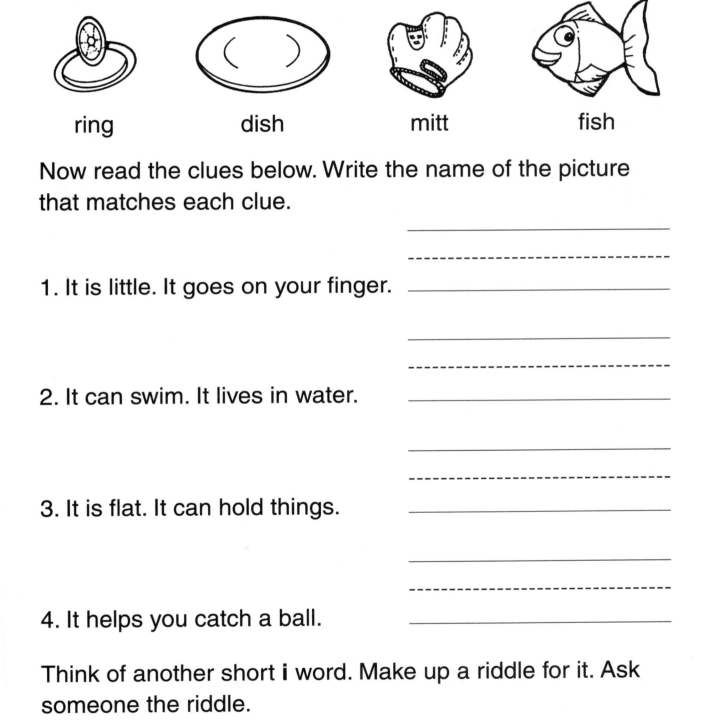

ring   dish   mitt   fish

Now read the clues below. Write the name of the picture that matches each clue.

1. It is little. It goes on your finger. _____

2. It can swim. It lives in water. _____

3. It is flat. It can hold things. _____

4. It helps you catch a ball. _____

Think of another short **i** word. Make up a riddle for it. Ask someone the riddle.

Short O Blocks

Write **o** on the lines and say the words you made. Listen to the short **o** sound in each word. Draw lines from the words on the blocks to the matching pictures.

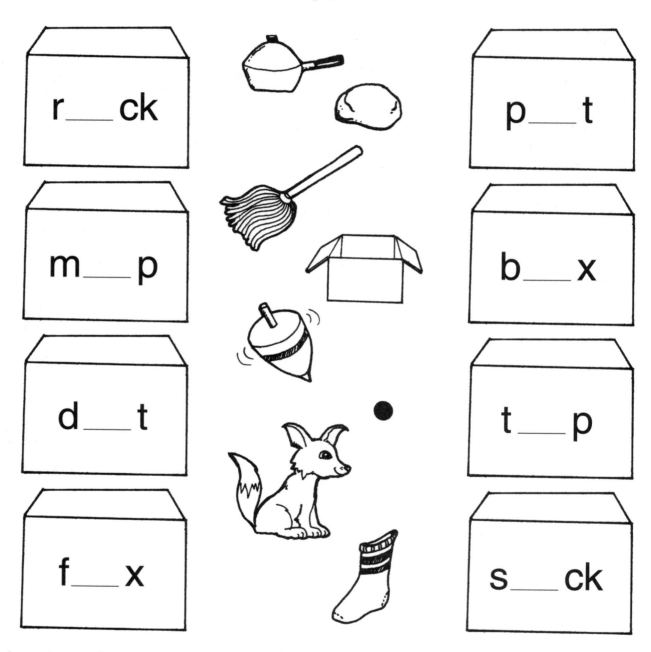

r___ck

p___t

m___p

b___x

d___t

t___p

f___x

s___ck

Look at the blocks again. Find the short **o** words that rhyme. Read them aloud.

In Scotty's Home

Scotty Doggie is looking around his home for things that have short **o** in their names. See what he has found so far. Draw at least three other things Scotty might find. Label your pictures.

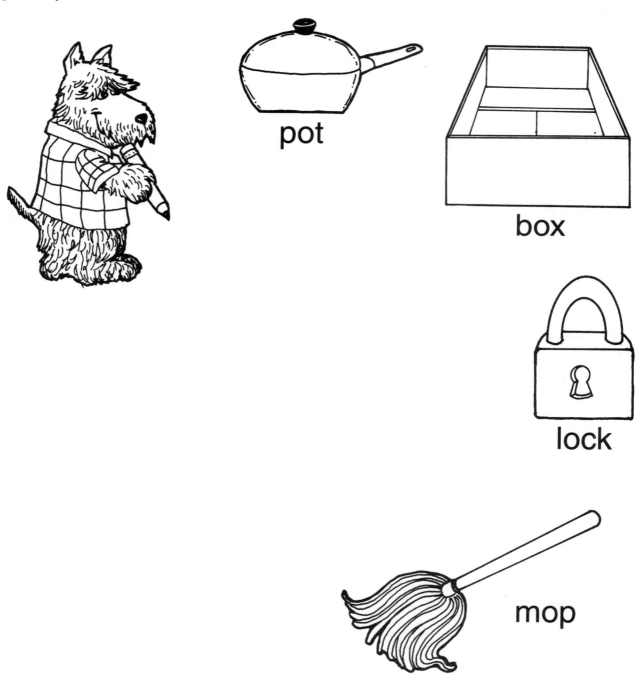

pot

box

lock

mop

Bud's Hut

Bud is going to his hut. The words **Bud** and **hut** have the short **u** sound. Help Bud get to his hut. Make a path by coloring the pictures that have short **u** in their names.

Buffy's Puzzle

Buffy wrote some short **u** words. Use them to label the pictures below. The shapes of the boxes will help you.

| bus | sun | rug |
| jug | bug | duck |

1.

2.

3.

4.

5.

6.

Clickety-Clack!

Look at the trains. Say the names of the pictures and listen for the short vowel sound. On each train, draw two more pictures with matching vowel sounds. Label the pictures.

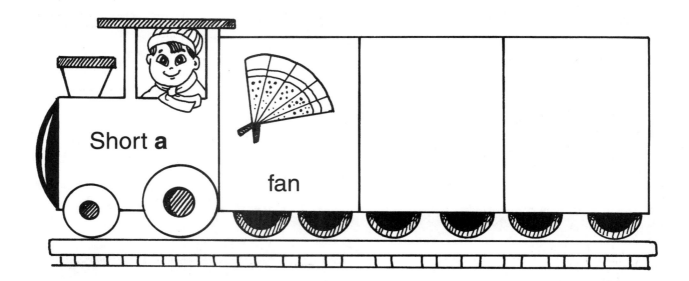

Short **a**

fan

Short **e**

bed

Short **i** — pin

Short **o** — sock

Short **u** — bug

Jake the Snake

Here is a snake named Jake. The words **snake** and **Jake** have the long **a** sound. Look at each picture on Jake. If the picture has long **a** in its name, color that part of Jake green. If not, color that part of Jake yellow.

Look at Jake's colors. Describe the pattern.

Can You?

Read the questions. Circle the long **a** words. Then answer the questions **yes** or **no**.

Can you write your name? _____

Can you help bake a cake? _____

Can you skate? _____

Can you wave good-bye? _____

Choose one of the questions to which you answered **yes**. Draw a picture showing what you can do.

Ride the Slides

Mike and Clive will ride the slides. Who will get to the bottom first? To find out, color the pictures that have the long **i** sound, as in **ride** and **slide**. The child on the slide with more colored pictures is the winner.

Who won? _____

Time for Fun

Read the sentences below to find out what the children are doing for fun. Circle any long **i** words you see. Then draw a line from each sentence to the matching picture.

Sara rides her bike.

Tim goes on a hike.

Sam goes down a slide.

Kim plays with her kite.

Mike plays hide-and-seek.

What do you like to do for fun? Try writing your answer. Then tell a parent or a friend what you like to do.

_____

- -

_____

At Joe's Home

Joe is at home working in his backyard. The words **Joe** and **home** have the long **o** sound. Look at the picture. Find six things that have long **o** in their names. Color them yellow.

Which two long **o** objects rhyme? Circle them.

Read and Match

Read the sentences and circle any long **o** words you see.
Underline the sentences that match the pictures.

The girl has a rose.

The girl has a note.

The dog dug a hole.

The dog got a pole.

The robe is long.

The rope is long.

The boy has a bone.

The boy has a cone.

Choose a sentence
you did not underline.
Draw a picture to
match it.

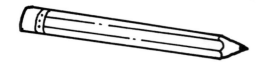

Julie's Presents

Julie had a birthday party in June. Look at the presents she got. Each one has the long **u** sound in its name, as in **Julie** and **June**. Write the names of the presents beside the matching pictures. Use the shapes of the boxes to help you.

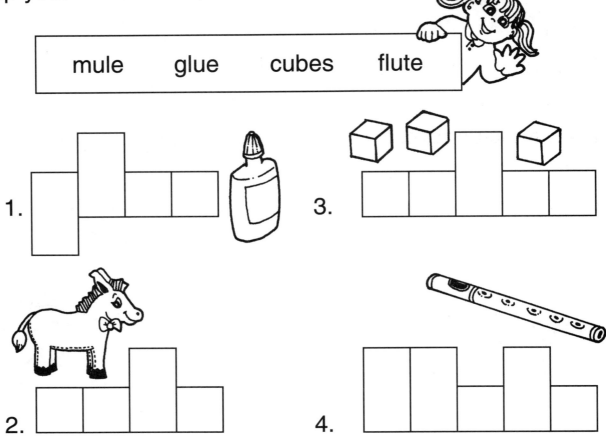

mule	glue	cubes	flute

1.

2.

3.

4.

Draw a present that you got. Tell why you liked it.

Long U Scavenger Hunt

Work with someone at home. Read the list below and circle any long **u** words you see. Then look around your home for the things on the list. Check off the items as you find them.

☐ a tube of toothpaste   ☐ a cute toy

☐ an ice cube   ☐ a flute

☐ a picture of a mule   ☐ a huge box

☐ something that plays a tune   ☐ something used for cooking

How many items did you find? _____
Tell where you found them.

How many items did you not find? _____
Tell where you think you might find them.

A Long Vowel Race

Find out who will win the race. Write **a, i, o,** or **u** on the lines to complete the words.

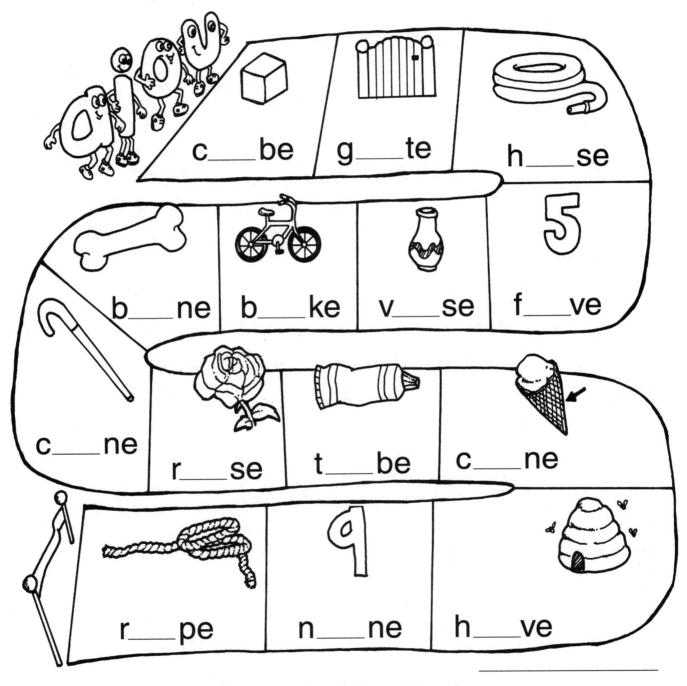

c___be   g___te   h___se

b___ne   b___ke   v___se   f___ve

c___ne

r___se   t___be   c___ne

r___pe   n___ne   h___ve

Which vowel won the race? (**Hint:** Which
vowel did you write the most times?)

_____

- - - - - - - - - - - - - - - - - - -

_____

56

Pete's Pictures

Pete drew some pictures of things that have long **e** in their names. Say the name of each picture. Listen to the long **e** sound. Then label the pictures using the words in the box.

feet	bee	meat	leaf
seal	beet	seed	teeth

Look at each pair of pictures. How are they alike?

Colorful Apples

Look at the words on the apples. If the apple has a word with a short vowel, color it red. If it has a word with a long vowel, color it green.

Name at least three things you can make with apples.

What a Shower!

Look at the picture on each raindrop. Say its name. Then complete the matching words below by writing in the missing letters.

1. | c | u | |

5. | c | | | e |

2. | | o | |

6. | | | n |

3. | w | | |

7. | k | | | e |

4. | | | s | e |

8. | | | k | e |

Word Makers

The machines below are Word Makers. You can make words with the letters that are on them. Combine two or more letters at a time to make words. Write them on the lines. See how many words you can make!

Answers

Page 9
These pictures and the bugs beside them should be colored: banana, bag, boot, book, ball. Pictures will vary.

Page 10

Cocoa is a cat.

Page 11
These pictures should be colored: dinosaur, desk, dice, drapes, dishes, dog, dog dish. Additional **d** pictures will vary. Examples: duck, door, drum.

Page 12
Parent: Child should draw 3 more fish, a fat fox, a funny face, and 3 more forks.

Page 13
1. game
2. gold
3. girl
4. grass
5. gate
6. grape

Page 14
These words should be circled: Harry, has, hat, his, head; He, has, hammer, his, hand; He, his, house.
Parent: Child's picture should reflect the meaning of the sentences.

Page 15
These words should be completed on the balls: jar, jam, jug, jet, jump.

Page 16

Page 17
Pictures will vary. Examples: lion, leaf, lock, lemon.

Page 18
mug   mitten
mask   moth

Page 19

Page 20
These pictures should be colored: parrot, penguin, pig, porcupine; peanuts, pear, pineapple, peas; paints, paintbrush, pencil, paper.
One pie shows pictures of animals; another pie shows pictures of things to eat; another pie shows pictures of things used for writing or drawing.

Page 21
queen – yes
house – no
quilt – yes
quarter – yes
ball – no
Questions will vary.

Page 22
These objects on the path should be circled: rope, rock, ruler, ribbon, rug, ring.
The ruler should be colored yellow.

Page 23
These words should be circled: Sue, six, socks; Some, socks, spots; Some, socks, stripes; socks, spots, socks, stripes.
Parent: Child should draw four socks with spots and two socks with stripes.

Page 24

These **t** things should be circled: towel, toothbrush, tube.

Page 25
van
vase
vest

Page 26
Pictures will vary. Examples: worm, watch, whale, window.

Page 27

Page 28

These words should be circled:
yak, Yogi; yellow; you, Yogi, Yak;
yummy.
Pictures will vary.

Page 29

These words should be circled:
Zeke, zebra; zoo; zippers.
Pictures will vary. Examples:
jacket, skirt, pants.

Page 30

top – t	kite – k	jacks – j
hat – h	pants – p	mitten – m
lion – l	fish – f	dog – d
van – v	boat – b	car – c

First row shows toys.
Second row shows things to wear.
Third row shows animals.
Fourth row shows things that go.

Page 32

doll – l	flag – g	sled – d
boat – t	drum – m	bus – s
top – p	balloon – n	duck – k

Pictures will vary.

Page 33

1. hen, van
2. log, pig
3. cat, pot
4. fox, box
Stories will vary.

Page 34

These words should be completed:
hat, bed, wig, mop, sun.

Page 35

Pictures will vary but may include
the following: dog or duck; cat or
rabbit; bread or banana; corn or
chicken; window; sink.

Page 36

These pictures should be
colored: cap, apple, lamp, mask,
bat.
The cap and mask should be
circled.

Page 37

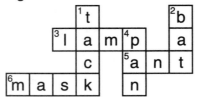

Page 38

Page 39

These words should be circled:
Brett; pet; pet, Fred; resting, bed.
Pictures will vary.

Page 40

The fish with these pictures
should be colored: king, wing,
ring; wig, pig; fin, pin.
The names of the colored
pictures on each dish are
rhyming words.

Page 41

1. ring
2. fish
3. dish
4. mitt
Riddles will vary.

Page 42

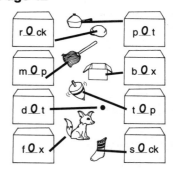

The rhyming pairs are: rock and
sock; mop and top; dot and pot;
fox and box.

Page 43

Pictures will vary but may include
the following: sock, doll, rock, top.

Page 44

Page 45

1. bug	4. jug
2. sun	5. bus
3. rug	6. duck

Pages 46–47

Pictures will vary.
Parent: Make sure child's
pictures match the vowel sound
on each train.

Page 48
These pictures should be colored green: cake, skate, plane, cane, tape, rake, cape, cave.
Jake has a green–green–yellow pattern that repeats.

Page 49
These words should be circled: name; bake, cake; skate; wave.
Answers and pictures will vary.

Page 50
These pictures on Mike's slide should be colored: pie, kite, ice, nine, bike.
These pictures on Clive's slide should be colored: five, fire, hive.
Mike won.

Page 51
These words should be circled: rides, bike; hike; slide; kite; Mike, hide.

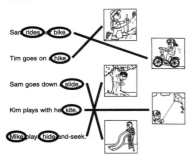

Answers to the question will vary.

Page 52

Hose and **rose** rhyme; those pictures should be circled.

Page 53
These words should be circled: rose, note, hole, pole, robe, rope, bone, cone.
These sentences should be underlined:
The girl has a rose.
The dog dug a hole.
The rope is long.
The boy has a cone.
Pictures will vary.

Page 54
1. glue   3. cubes
2. mule   4. flute
Pictures will vary.

Page 55
These words should be circled: tube, cute, cube, flute, mule, huge, tune, used.
Rest of answer will vary.

Page 56
These words should be completed on the path: cube, gate, hose, five, vase, bike, bone, cane, rose, tube, cone, hive, nine, rope.
The vowel **o** won the race.

Page 57

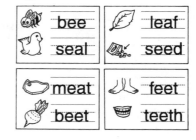

Suggested answers to question: the bee and seal are animals; the leaf and seeds are things that grow; the meat and beet are food items; the feet and mouth are parts of the body.

Page 58
The apples with these words should be colored red: cap, pin, top, tub, lamp, net, nut.
The apples with these words should be colored green: hike, hole, cape, seal, tube, bake, feet, rope, five.
Examples of things made with apples: pies, cakes, applesauce, muffins.

Page 59
1. cup   5. cube
2. top   6. fan
3. web   7. kite
4. rose   8. rake

Page 60
These are some of the words that can be made from each machine:
bike, bake, lake, like, leak, beak
man, ten, tan, net, mat, meat, team
top, hop, pet, hope, pot, the

Other

books that will help develop your child's gifts and talents

Workbooks:

- Reading (4–6) $4.95
- Reading Book Two (4–6) $4.95
- Math (4–6) $4.95
- Math Book Two (4–6) $4.95
- Language Arts (4–6) $4.95
- Language Arts Puzzles & Games (4–6) $4.95
- Puzzles & Games for
  Reading and Math (4–6) $4.95
- Puzzles & Games for
  Reading and Math Book Two (4–6) $4.95
- Puzzles & Games for
  Critical and Creative Thinking (4–6) $4.95
- Phonics (4–6) $4.95
- Phonics Book Two (4–6) $4.95
- Phonics Puzzles & Games (4–6) $4.95
- Math Puzzles & Games (4–6) $4.95
- Reading Puzzles & Games (4–6) $4.95

For orders, call 1-800-323-4900.

Science Workbooks:

- The Human Body (4–6) $5.95
- Animals (4–6) $5.95
- The Earth (4–6) $5.95
- The Ocean (4–6) $5.95

Question & Answer Books:

- The Gifted & Talented® Question &
  Answer Book for Ages 4–6 $5.95
- Gifted & Talented® More Questions &
  Answers for Ages 4–6 $5.95
- Gifted & Talented® Still More Questions
  & Answers for Ages 4–6 $5.95
- Gifted & Talented® Questions & Answers
  Super Edition for Ages 4–6 $9.95